Teachers

Quinn M. Arnold

CREATIVE EDUCATION • CREATIVE PAPERBACKS

seedlings

Published by Creative Education and Creative Paperbacks
P.O. Box 227, Mankato, Minnesota 56002
Creative Education and Creative Paperbacks
are imprints of The Creative Company
www.thecreativecompany.us

Design by Ellen Huber; production by Christine Vanderbeek
Art direction by Rita Marshall
Printed in the United States of America

Photographs by Alamy (Michael Dwyer, Lynnette
Peizer), iStockphoto (asiseeit, IPGGutenbergUKLtd,
monkeybusinessimages, percds), Shutterstock
(AlexeiLogvinovich, antoniodiaz, Emil Durov, ESB
Professional, littleny, Maglara, Jordi Muray, Picsfive, Olga
Popova, SpeedKingz, Alex Staroseltsev, wavebreakmedia)

Library of Congress Cataloging-in-Publication Data
Names: Arnold, Quinn M., author.
Title: Teachers / Quinn M. Arnold.
Series: Seedlings.
Includes bibliographical references and index.
Summary: A kindergarten-level introduction to teachers,
covering their job description, the places where they
work, and how they help the community by using their
instructional skills.
Identifiers: LCCN 2016059800
ISBN 978-1-60818-875-8 (hardcover)
ISBN 978-1-62832-490-7 (pbk)
ISBN 978-1-56660-923-4 (eBook)
Subjects: LCSH: Teachers—Juvenile literature.
Classification: LCC LB1775.A72 2017 / DDC 371.1—dc23
CCSS: RI.K.1, 2, 3, 4, 5, 6, 7;
RI.1.1, 2, 3, 4, 5, 6, 7; RF.K.1, 3; RF.1.1

First Edition HC 9 8 7 6 5 4 3 2 1
PBK 9 8 7 6 5 4 3 2

TABLE OF CONTENTS

Hello, teachers!

Teachers explain many subjects. They show how to do math and science.

They teach reading and writing.

Most teachers work in schools.

Some work in homes.

Teachers find ways to help children learn.

Teachers give homework and tests. These help them track how students learn.

Teachers fill out report cards. Parents meet with teachers.

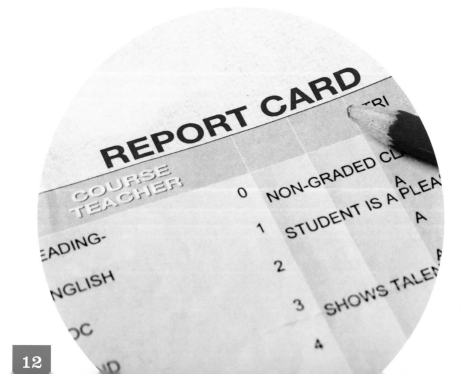

They talk about how their children are doing in class.

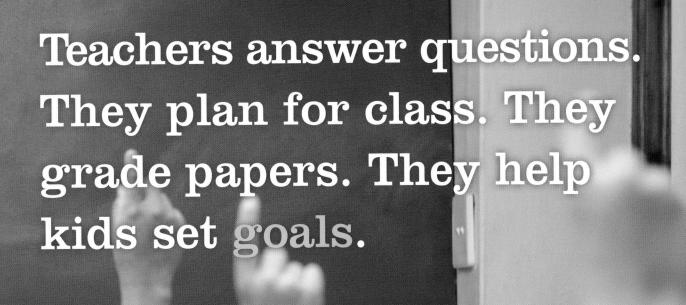

Teachers answer questions. They plan for class. They grade papers. They help kids set goals.

Teachers help students learn new things. They educate children in their community.

Goodbye, teachers!

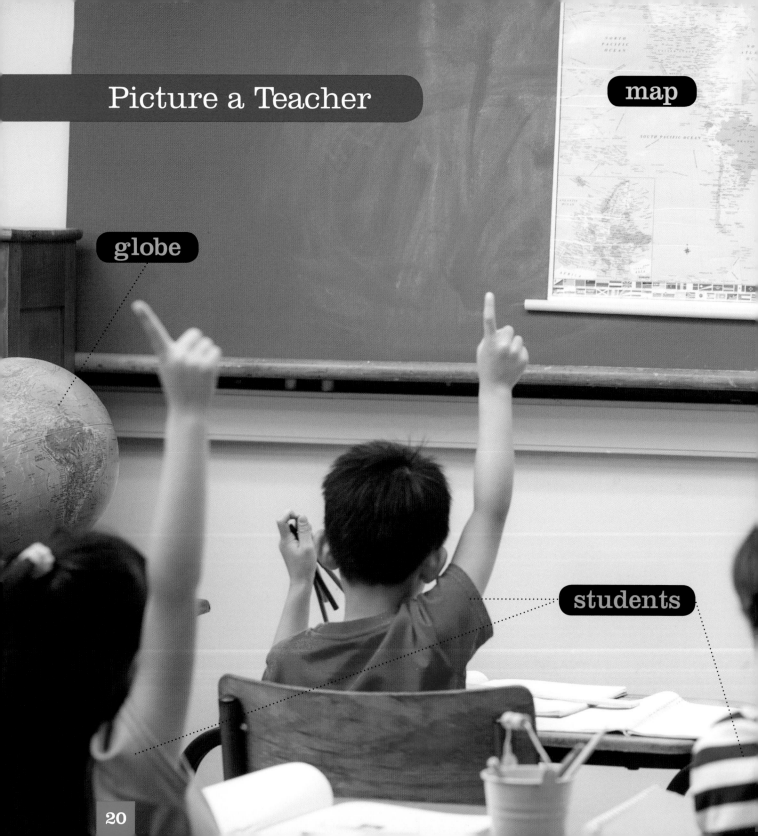

Picture a Teacher

map

globe

students

chalkboard

teacher

goals: things to be done or accomplished

subjects: topics studied in school, like math, science, or history

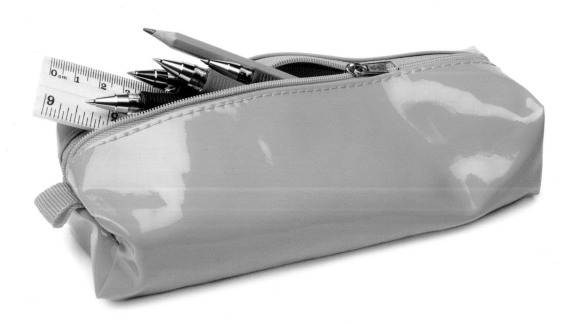

Read More

Kidde, Rita. *What Do Teachers Do?*
New York: PowerKids Press, 2015.

Meister, Cari. *Teachers.*
Minneapolis: Jump!, 2014.

Websites

KidsHealth: What Makes a Great Teacher
http://kidshealth.org/en/kids/great-teacher.html?WT.ac=ctg
Find out what makes a good teacher—according to kids!

Super Coloring: Professions Coloring Pages
http://www.supercoloring.com/coloring-pages/people
/professions
Find pictures of teachers, and print them out to color.

Index